AF589354

This book is dedicated to
my granddaughter, Meyla Eve.

May you always find joy in your own
unique voice and whistle through life with
love, laughter, and confidence.

This book is for you and for all
the little whistlers out there.

–**LL**

Illustrated by Kat Powell | Book design by Jodi McPhee

ISBN (Hard cover): 979-8-9933837-0-5
ISBN (Paperback): 979-8-9933837-1-2
ISBN (eBook): 979-8-9933837-2-9

Library of Congress Control Number: 2026903215

Printed in the United States

The Magical Teapot Party

By Leslie Lilien

Illustrated by Kat Powell

I can't go. I **JUSSST** can't go," Camille sobbed and whistled at the same time. All her crying made her eyes swell up.

As the clock struck three, Camille realized there were only three more hours left until the Second Annual Teapot Party would begin, a party Camille had been waiting for all year. That was, until that fateful moment the week before, when, while rushing about, she forgot to turn on the light and toppled into her tea cart and chipped her spout.

TEA

Her eyes slowly closed, and she began dreaming about how exciting and how much fun her first teapot gala was! It was so magnificent, so mesmerizing, and so very colorful too!

Camille's eyes had widened in amazement when she saw the most fabulous teapots in all shapes and sizes from countries around the world—including France, Italy, Holland, Japan, Slovakia, Greece, and Israel. There were clay pots, fine porcelain china, shiny brass kettles, hand-painted ceramic teapots, even glass. There were houses, cows, fish, even a bearded gnome if you could believe it. Every design imaginable was at this marvelous event.

I Have a
Little Dreidel

Then, from out of the crowd, a dashing Delft teapot, with eyes as blue as the sky and a handlebar mustache, glided toward her. He tipped his lid and bowed.

“Hello, I am Van Baron… of Friesland… from Holland.”

“I am Camille of Edbern… um… New Jersey,” she said shyly.

“Camille, may I have this dance?”

“Yes, you,” and before she could say the word “may,” Van Baron swooped her onto the beautiful black and white diamond dance floor that gleamed under the sparkling chandelier.

Hooking handles, Camille and Van Baron were swept into the spinning crowd, laughing and singing along with the band with high-pitched **wheeeeeeees**!

When the band announced their last song, Camille was a little sad knowing the night had to end. It was such a magical moment, she felt like Cinderella. Smiling at Van Baron, she said, "Thank you. I had a wonderful time."

"I did too! Meet me here! Same time next year," Van Baron whispered to Camille....

Tea Tones

At that moment, while she was still dreaming, the cupboard opened, and Sally, the sugar bowl, leapt out and began to call to her: "Camille... Camille... Camille... wake up... wake up!"

Camille nearly toppled off the teacart. Sally grabbed her spout just in time. “I’m sorry. I didn’t mean to startle you. You need to get ready. You don’t want to be late for the party.”

“I can’t go,” Camille whistled.

“What are you saying?” Sally’s eyes widened in dismay. “You have been talking about nothing else for a whole year.”

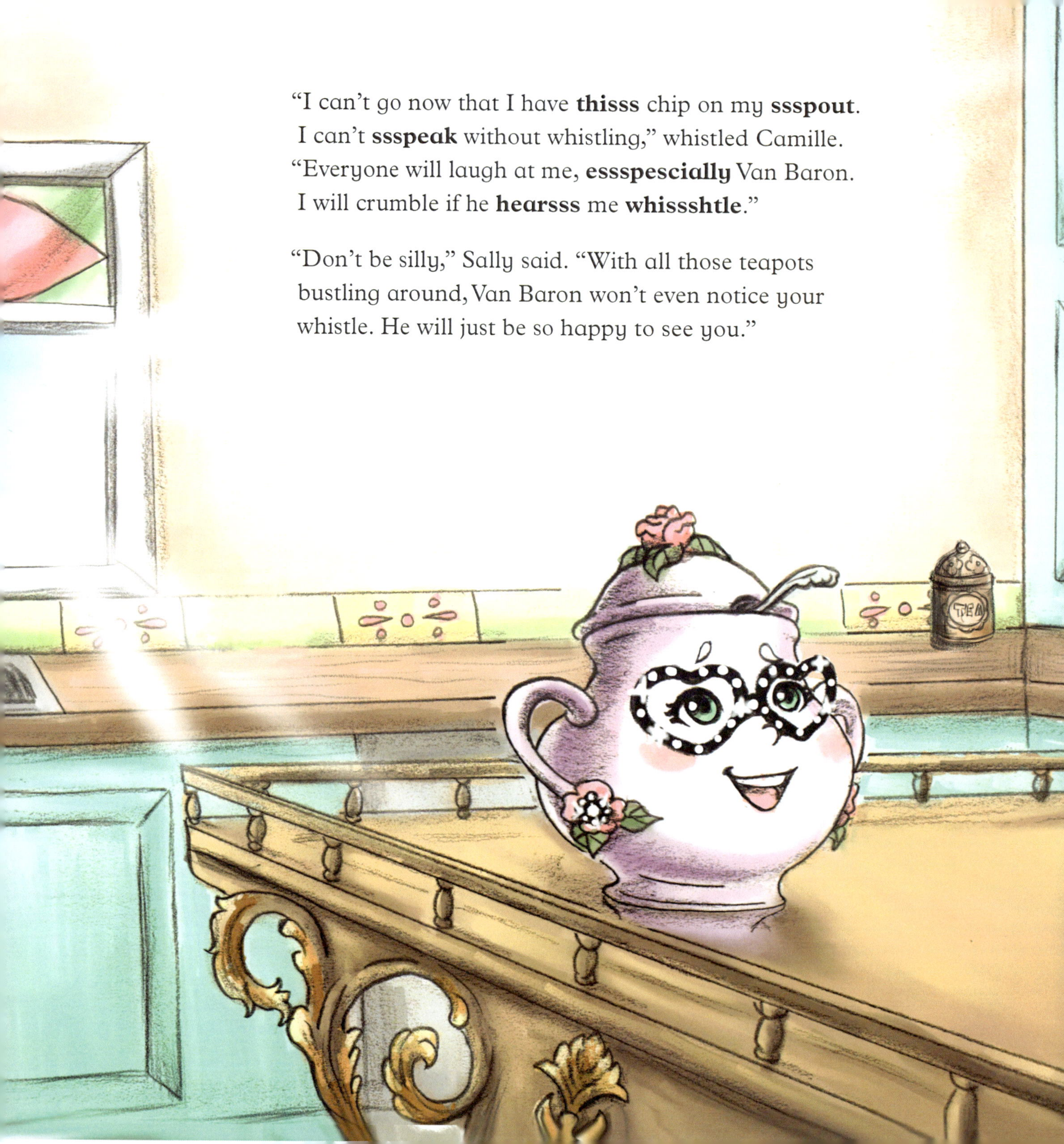

"I can't go now that I have **thisss** chip on my **ssspout**. I can't **ssspeak** without whistling," whistled Camille. "Everyone will laugh at me, **essspescially** Van Baron. I will crumble if he **hearsss** me **whissshtle**."

"Don't be silly," Sally said. "With all those teapots bustling around, Van Baron won't even notice your whistle. He will just be so happy to see you."

"Everyone has imperfections," Sally assured her. "We all have something that we don't like about ourselves. Look at me, for instance. I have four eyes!" she said, laughing. "When I found out I needed to wear glasses all the time, I wanted to hide."

"But your **glasssesss** make your beautiful **eyesss** even bigger," Camille whistled.

"And your chip gives you character! It makes you sound like only you can sound. It makes you, **YOU**—and everyone who loves you, loves your whistle too.

"Just focus on all of your good qualities, and remember, there is a lid for every teapot," sparkled Sally.

“**Thankssss** for being my **bessstest** friend, **Sssally**,” Camille said with a whistle in her voice.

“Now go and get ready, or you will miss the party!” Sally ordered Camille with a knowing grin.

Camille smiled as she spotted her reflection in the mirrored glass cupboard door. She saw her pretty polka-dotted yellow kettle. She loved her fancy butterfly on her hat and black and white striped handle and matching spout. But when her powder puff caught on her chip, that was all she could see.

Camille wanted to believe Sally's words, but she still felt uncomfortable.

"I've got it!" she exclaimed. "I will go to the party but not **ssspeak**! That way, no one will hear my **whissstle**."

Camille then rushed to get ready. She wanted to get to the party right on time to blend in with the arriving crowd.

At six o'clock sharp, Camille entered the hall, trying not to be conspicuous. She quickly slid in between a tall, sleek, shiny brass teapot from Turkey and a porcelain, snow-covered house teapot with a snowman on its porch.

Camille was awestruck by the glittering chandelier, the royal purple walls, and bright, polished floor. It was even more spectacular than she remembered.

I Have a
Little Dreidel

While scanning the crowd, she saw a beautiful, porcelain, Japanese pagoda teapot and an adorable, hand-painted, ceramic cow teapot with a bright red scarf and a chicken on his lid standing near the dessert cart.

Tones

Suddenly, the bustling crowd went silent. Everyone turned to look right.

The new arrival was the most magnificent teapot Camille had ever seen. She wore an ivory gown bedazzled with stunning, famous Capodimonte flowers and entwining vines of leaves.

"That is the Duchess of Capodimonte, of Naples, Italy," she overheard a teapot next to her whisper.

"**Isssnt ssshe Eksssquisssit**!" Camille's whistle gushed out.

"Oh no!" Camille's face turned beet red, like a teapot boiling over. She had broken her vow not to speak, and now her whistle echoed across the room like six teakettles on a stove whistling frantically at the same time.

Every teapot turned and stared at her. Even the Duchess shot a glance her way. Camille wanted to crawl into a hole and hide.

“Camille. Camille, **isss** that you?”

“Uh-oh!” What now?” Camille panicked.

“Camille, **iths isss** I,” whistled the voice.

Still shaken by her outburst, she willed herself to turn around.

Standing before her, with his cream colored suit trimmed with delph blue and his handlebar mustache upswept in a smile, was Van Baron!

"Camille, I am **sssoo** happy to **ssssee** you," he whistled.

Wait...was that a whistle she heard? She lifted her eyes slowly. Then she saw it: there it was, a small chip missing from his spout.

"I wasss afraid you'd **notisssce**," he said with a faint whistle, as he saw her staring at his spout. "I bumped **againssst** a cabinet."

"I have one too!" Camille whistled, half smiling.

They both burst out laughing and lifted their spouts to the sky with one long whistle.

“If you are not **t-t-too em-b-barras-s-s-sed** to be **s-s-seen** with **m-m-me**,” Van Baron whistled, “may I have **thisss danccce**?”

"**Yesss,**" Camille whistled.

"**Thisss isss abssthhsssolutely** wonderful," Van Baron declared, his spout whistling with joy.

Tea Tones

For the rest of the night, Camille and Van Baron laughed, danced, sang, and whistled with all of their friends from around the world in harmony.

See you at the next teapot party!

Author's Note and How to Whistle

Whistles, people, and teapots have something in common—they all come in different shapes, colors, and sizes, each with a unique purpose. As a child, I struggled with certain sounds, especially S's and L's. My S's even whistled when I spoke, and speech therapy helped me find my voice. That experience taught me that differences aren't flaws—they're simply part of who we are.

In *The Magical Teapot Party*, Camille is a teapot whose whistle makes her feel different—until she discovers that her unique sound has a special purpose. Her story reflects what I've learned through teaching, parenting, and storytelling: when children are encouraged to embrace what makes them unique, confidence can grow.

This book is for every child finding their voice, for the parents and teachers guiding them, and for anyone learning to accept their own little imperfections. Life isn't about being perfect—it's about whistling through it, appreciating beauty, good friends, and the unique sounds we all bring into the world.

Teaching a child to whistle is like teaching them to tie their shoes or ride a bike— grown-ups do it without thinking, but it can be tricky to learn! Whistling isn't just for calling dogs—it's fun and can help with speech, communication, and even music. Ready to try?

Steps:

- Pucker your lips like a small kiss.
- Blow air softly—you might hear a faint tone.
- Blow a little harder while keeping your tongue curled.
- Adjust your lips slightly to change the sound.
- Try different tones, then whistle a song!

Note to Parents and Teachers

Let children hear a simple whistle first. Show them how to curl their tongue into a U-shape and gently push their lips forward. Encourage playful practice. They may stop and start, and that's okay. With patience, guidance, and gentle reminders, the whistle will come—and it will be fun!

–**Leslie Lilien**

Acknowledgments

To my friends, who listened to my endless ideas about whistling teapots and never told me to put a lid on it—your love and encouragement mean the world to me.

With gratitude to the educators, speech pathologists, and parents who shared their insights and reinforced the importance of play in learning.

Special thanks to Whitney, my first little reader.

And finally, to the parents, teachers, and children who will read this story—may you find joy in every whistle, just as I have.

Special Acknowledgments

With sincere thanks to illustrator Kat Powell and designer Jodi McPhee for bringing *The Magical Teapot Party* to life.

–**Leslie Lilien**

About the Author

Leslie Lilien is a mother, grandmother, and preschool teacher. As a child, she even whistled when she spoke! *The Magical Teapot Party* is her debut picture book, inspired by helping children find their own voices.

About the Illustrator

Kat Powell is a freelance illustrator and fine artist with a BFA in Studio Art from Texas Tech University. She loves creating vibrant artwork and has illustrated children's books, young adult books, and graphic novels.

www.ingramcontent.com/pod-product-compliance
Ingram Content Group UK Ltd.
Pitfield, Milton Keynes, MK11 3LW, UK
UKRC032027290726
14090UKWH00008B/486

* 9 7 9 8 9 9 3 3 8 3 7 1 2 *

9 798993 383712